THE ROCKET

Written by Paul Shipton

Illustrated by Pet Gotohda

Bish, Bash and Bosh were at
the shops.
They had to avoid the big feet!

2

This planet is hard work!

Bash wanted to join his friends in the stars.

Perhaps you will get your wish!

Bish pointed at a rocket. She had a clever plan.

4

The rocket had a slot for a coin.

"Sorted!" cried Bish.

"Here is a coin by the kerb!"

It was hard work to hoist the coin up.

At last they got the coin in
the slot.

The rocket started, but it just
rocked a bit.
Then it stopped.

"That was short," snarled Bash.
"After all that hard work, we are
still here!"

Oi! Down here!

"I'm not," said Bosh.
Bish and Bash peeped over.

"I can see stars," said Bosh.
"Come and join me!"